Going Like Lynn is written for women who have a yen to travel — those who have always wanted to go, have almost gone, or are finally ready to travel for pure pleasure.

My serious traveling began on my 30th birthday. I thought I was meeting my significant other, who lived in San Francisco. We were planning to travel in California together. When he called with a million and one excuses why he could not meet me, I was livid and decided to show him that I could have a lovely holiday without him.

After conferring with a travel agent, who told me how booked up Europe, the United States and Canada were, I picked Yucatan from a world map hanging in the office. The agent had to call Pan Am to see how to get there. I left with $500 dollars in traveler's checks, a charge card, a Spanish-English dictionary, and a small carry-on case. I knew I was headed for a wonderful new adventure. I was utterly and completely fearless and in my excitement, even forgot about my significant other.

In the long run, that first major solo trip became much more important in my life than my significant other. Yucatan was my entry into the world of travel and I have been hooked ever since. I am the most sophisticated poor person you will ever meet and spend every penny on travel. I have never owned a V.C.R., microwave oven or dishwasher. My furniture is hand-me-down, but my life is the fullest of anyone I know. I have had dinner with descendants of kings, peasants and slaves. Each encounter has enriched me.

I hope to touch something in and give courage to every woman who picks up this book. For those who are ready to go, this book could be the catalyst.

**From one traveler to another,
Bon Voyage
and Happy Journeys.**

Lynn Portnoy

*With heartfelt thanks to a special friend
and invaluable editor, Judy Bobrow and
designer, Lisa Hajnal of Grigg Graphic Services, Inc.
who helped bring this book to life.*

First Printing – January 1999
Second Printing – April 1999

Table of Contents

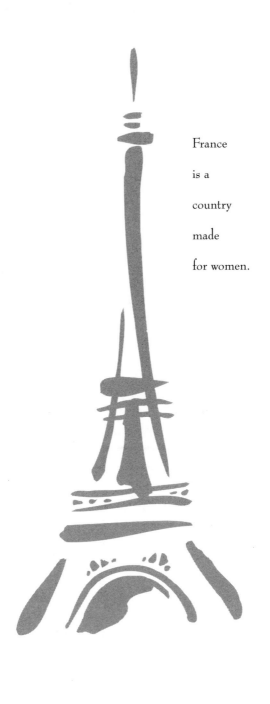

France

is a

country

made

for women.

Why Paris?

Historically, our ideas about fashion have come from the French. Shopping is still a national pastime. A perfectly groomed, well-dressed woman with just the right scarf or piece of jewelry is admired equally by men and women. French women exude style and simple understated elegance. Paris is a perfect place for American women to experiment with creating their own chic look by just buying a fabulous scarf. If you appreciate art, antiques and architecture; love history and culture; enjoy gracious living; and are an enthusiastic person France is like heaven waiting for your discovery.

Besides fashion and culture, the greatest indoor-outdoor pastime in France is dining. This is a nation that is passionate about food. From the marketing, preparation and presentation — to the consumption, cuisine is an integral part of the culture.

The French will automatically accept you if you show proper enthusiasm and respect for a fine meal. Talking about food is a great way to begin a conversation. Describing what someone has ordered, eaten, or is about to consume at the next table, is a perfect ice breaker. Even asking at a small cafe for a recommendation of a good, inexpensive nearby restaurant, will start a lively conversation between patrons, waiters and the proprietor about the various merits of all the neighboring establishments.

If you don't speak a word of French, come prepared with a phrase book, a map, a list of restaurants (with phone numbers and addresses) and a green Michelin (the authoritative guide book for France). Don't worry about a lack of language skills. In the large cities like Paris, most people can speak some English. The hotel concierges and waiters all speak English.

If you are traveling in the countryside, someone will assist you by pantomime or help you find someone who speaks English. Remember a map or a card with an address will elicit instant understanding and assistance. Do not hesitate to have your concierge write everything out for you every morning. Your list should include: Metro (French subway) directions; the names and sizes of items you wish to purchase; and the names and addresses of shops, museums, monuments, parks and restaurants you wish to visit.

I have never met an American who got permanently lost in France and was unable to return home or to his or her hotel, or to eat or drink, because of an inability to speak French. The fear of mishaps because you cannot speak another language is a million times worse than the reality. Columbus found America—surely you can find your hotel.

If you think about it, dogs and cats get everything they want without speaking. They eat, go out, pee and get their tummies rubbed—all without saying one word of people language. And we all understand them perfectly. With a bit of luck and a friendly, non-judgmental manner, someone will understand your needs. Just be open to cultural differences and keep your sense of humor about unavoidable comic mishaps.

The great fun

of traveling

for me

is not knowing

exactly what

to expect next.

A Slight Mishap

PARDON MY BLOOPER

The great fun of traveling for me is not knowing exactly what to expect next. I love to have two or three days totally unplanned on every trip, when I can just meander. You cannot get lost because there is no place you really have to be! The freedom of doing exactly what you want to do, when you want to do it, is a luxury for most of us.

On one of my first trips to France, I rented a car for three days in Avignon. Since I had never been there, it did not matter which road I took. It was all new to me. I ended up in Haute Provence at the Gorges du Verdon, a small-scale version of the Grand Canyon. What an unexpected thrill to come across this splendiferous site on a little back road. (If only I were not terrified of heights!)

After following another small road for an hour, I found an 18th century chateau (hotel) in semi-dilapidation. Madame, the proprietress, was in her 80s and showed me to a vast room where I expected the king, queen and entire royal court of France to receive me. The room was enormous with high ceilings and a magnificent chandelier. The twin beds and windows were covered in fraying rose silk satin and the furniture was exquisite — probably placed there in the 18th century and not moved since.

My room (including both dinner and breakfast) was about $38. I thanked Madame and took my overnight bag upstairs. I looked in my bathroom and found a large spider family assembled in the old rusted tub. So much for my bath. I turned on the water in the sink and what dribbled out was a vivid russet. Next I sat on the bed and the springs greeted me with some unusual sounds as well as terrific lilting movements.

The chateau was built on a hilltop. From my window I could see a clear small lake about a mile below the house. I changed into my swimsuit, big shirt and baggy pants and followed the track down to the little lake. I rested on the shore and the afternoon sun grew hotter and hotter. It was time to cool off.

Slowly I waded into the cool fresh water. The lake was calm and delicious and I swam for about 20 minutes. I returned to the shore where I dozed off, completely relaxed! The sound of an old truck awakened me. It was the young local farmer who helped Madame at the chateau. He was returning from a nearby village where he had purchased meat and bread for din-

ner. He was more than a little surprised to
find me in a wet bathing suit. I was aston-
ished to discover that this beautiful little
lake was a reservoir.

That evening over a delicious dinner
with lots of wine, Madame and a few guests
thoroughly enjoyed a hearty laugh on my
mistaking the reservoir for a lake. Need-
less to say, none of the guests touched
their water glasses! My *faux pas* (blooper)
was certainly part of the evening's
entertainment.

My whole 24-hour stay at the fairy-tale
castle was like being in a time machine.
I was not lost from anywhere, but had
found myself happily suspended between
the 18th and 20th centuries through a
serendipitous happening that will live on
as a delightful memory! My slight mishap
became the highlight of my trip.

> Mishaps will eventually
> enhance the memory of your trip,
> ending up as highlights.

How To's
for a One-Week
to Ten-Day Trip to Paris

✔ Planning, packing
  and air travel

✔ French Government
  Tourist Office

✔ Decide itinerary
  and dates

✔ Select hotels

✔ Book airline tickets,
  local transportation
  and tours.

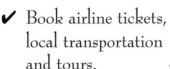

✔ Read guide books,
  brochures and
  travel articles.

Planning

➤ Buy a wallet-size notebook and a small journal.

➤ Have passport photos taken and obtain a passport application at the post office. Most automobile clubs offer the passport photo service as well as camera shops. Check your local Yellow Pages. Complete and bring back application with photos to the post office. Jot down the date that you returned the forms to the post office in your notebook.

➤ Put your credit card numbers and driver's license number in your notebook (without your name). Remember to note the expiration dates and the credit card emergency numbers (both domestic and international) to call if lost or stolen. When you receive your passport, record the passport number, date, city where issued, and date of expiration in your notebook. Also, make three photocopies of the first two pages (your picture along with the passport number). Give one copy to a family member or close friend; Put one copy in your cosmetic case; Keep one copy in your notebook.

➤ Book transportation. Call your travel agent for the best fares and connections. If needed, book local transportation–car rental, train ticket. When you receive

your airline tickets, record in your notebook your airline ticket number (you
will need the ticket number if lost),
airline flight numbers and dates, local
transportation–train ticket or car reservation confirmation numbers.

➢ Call or fax the hotel for reservations. Be
sure to request a brochure or a card from
the hotel, hopefully with a map or directions. Record your reservation confirmation numbers, the name and date of the
person who made the reservation, dates
reserved and the price of the room quoted. Don't forget to note the hotel name,
address, arrondissement (zip code) and
phone number in your notebook!!

➢ When traveling abroad, write down the
nearest phone number and address of
the **American Embassy** or consulate of
countries you will be visiting. Call the
U.S. State Department in Washington for
the telephone numbers. For Paris, the
number is **01-42-96-12-02.**

➢ Purchase travel health insurance for
abroad and trip cancellation insurance
from your travel agent and record the
policy number and emergency phone
number.

➢ Order foreign currency from your bank
two to three weeks before your tip. It is a
good idea to have the franc equivalent of
$150 to $200 on hand when you arrive.

➤ Write down names of two close friends or family members including home and business telephone numbers.

➤ Record medical information, including all generic names and dosages of prescription drugs, eyeglass or contact lens prescriptions, name and telephone number of your physicians (especially if you have a chronic illness) and allergies to foods and drugs such as penicillin.

➤ After purchasing traveler's checks, record denominations and serial numbers.

➤ Make sure you have an available credit card limit of at least $2,000 for any unforseen emergency.

➤ Give a copy of your completed itinerary, airline flight numbers and dates, hotel telephone and fax numbers (with area dialing codes) to a family member, coworker or good friend. Someone should always know where you are!!

➤ Read your guidebooks and travel literature on the area.

➤ Write in your notebook all the things you must see and do, and the names, addresses, telephone numbers and business hours of restaurants from all of your tour books, articles, brochures and friends' recommendations. Someone might even give you the name of a friend to call.

Traveling with One Bag

The trick to traveling with one bag is not the packing but again, the planning. Start with shopping for good classic basics that are seasonless. Fabrics like wool crepes and gabardines, good silks, the new synthetics that don't wrinkle, light-weight knits that can be layered, all work well for packing.

Many women find they must pack for a variety of weather on the same trip. Start with a good raincoat that is durable as well as packable. The armhole should be large enough to accommodate a heavy jacket or sweater sleeve. Wear your heavy jacket and coat on the plane. Plan on working with a two-or three-color wardrobe plus accents in scarves, blouses or sweaters.

13

Packing for a Seven-Day Trip

BASICS

➤ 3 bottoms (either pants or skirts) plus the one you are wearing.

➤ 1 jacket, blazer, suit jacket or cardigan sweater plus the one you are wearing. Be sure the two jackets work with the bottoms and tops.

➤ 6 tops (sweaters, blouses, T-shirts) plus the one you are wearing.

➤ 2 pairs of shoes–one pair of dress shoes and one pair of walking shoes– plus the pair you are wearing. Are your shoes all comfortable? Remember if your feet hurt, a trip can be ruined!

➤ Don't forget to pack a plastic skirt hanger. Many hotels still do not have skirt hangers. (Also handy for hanging pants or skirts in the shower to steam out the wrinkles.

➤ Underwear–3 sets, plus the set you are wearing.

➤ Light-weight fold-up nylon robe and nightgown or use a big T-shirt for sleeping and wear your raincoat for a robe.

ACCESSORIES

➤ A strand of faux pearls and pearl earrings to dress up any outfit and a simple faux gold or silver pin or necklace and earrings.

➤ A small flat purse for dinner or theatre.

➤ Silk or chiffon scarves to brighten your basic solid outfits.

➤ Cosmetics and make-up miniatures: Buy samples in grocery and drug stores. Keep one small case in your purse (travel toothbrush and toothpaste, deodorant, small washcloth, soap, miniature cleansing cream, hand lotion or Vaseline and your regular medications). Also include basic make-up, a small hairbrush and anything that will help you survive checked lost luggage, along with a change of underwear and a fresh top.

➤ Any additional personal items such as a small flashlight, that will add to your confidence.

Air Travel

→ Join an airline frequent flier program. The points add up to free airline tickets.

→ Use a credit card that gives you frequent flier points on your airline program. You can acquire many more points by charging all your regular monthly purchases on your card. (I even charge my groceries.)

→ If you are planning to travel frequently for business or pleasure, join an airline club. Choose the airline that has the best schedules for you. The clubs offer a faster way to check in. Clubs have a more comfortable, pleasant lounge where you can enjoy a complimentary cold drink or coffee before your flight. Away from the noise of overcrowded terminals, clubs have telephones and fax facilities and generally help reduce travel stress.

→ Wear comfortable, low-heeled walking shoes to get around the airport. The only good thing about the distances is you are burning up calories.

➧ Avoid alcohol. It does not mix with flying and one or two drinks can leave you
disoriented.

➧ Try to take nonstop flights when possible. If you need to change planes, allow
plenty of extra time. This will eliminate
the need to run through the airport like
a maniac to make your connection.

➧ Have a fast-reading paperback in your
purse to absorb you during the long
waits in airports, on runways and
while flying.

➧ Upgrade to business or first-class when
you can. Most carriers, however, have
changed their policies making upgrades
costly. So try for bulkhead seats in
coach, as close to the front as possible
and on either of the side sections. They
have more room than the center section,
which can be claustrophobic.

➧ Ask your travel agent or hotel to arrange
for transportation from the airport, especially if you are arriving at rush hour.

➧ Keep alcohol and coffee intake modest
on your first day. Eat simple grilled or
poached foods. Jet lag, rich foods and
alcohol don't mix well.

LUGGAGE

✈ Call your airline for its exact allowable
  measurements.

✈ Use a durable, light but strong, soft gar-
  ment bag or small carry-on. If you
  choose the right light-weight fabrics, all
  the pieces can easily be packed in the
  one bag of your choice and you will
  look like a smart well-dressed woman.

✈ For checked baggage, tie two bright rib-
  bons on your bag for quick recognition.

✈ And most important, wear a small
  wallet card case on a long strap around
  your neck, under your jacket for safety.
  You can also choose a small pouch to
  wear around your waist. I recommend
  wearing it on the plane and placing
  it in your carry-on bag during the
  evening flight.

The French Government Tourist Office

is so helpful that it is

a must for every

female traveler to France.

French Government Tourist Office

➤ This office is one of the best resources in planning your trip to Paris. It is funded by the French government to attract and assist travelers to France. (Tourism is a major part of the French economy.)

➤ You can request free, as well as moderately priced, hotel, restaurant and general tourist guides for any region in France.

➤ Free information on current cultural events and exhibitions is also available.

➤ Be sure to request a free copy of LaVie de Chateau, a group of large private homes in France that accept paying guests. They generally have three to six guestrooms and often you dine with the family and other guests. The guide lists prices, facilities available (such as dinner, swimming pool and horseback riding) and languages spoken. Almost all hosts speak English.

➤ In Paris, the French Tourist office on the Champs-Elysée, near the Arc de Triomphe, sells museum passes for one, three or five days for more than 30 museums and monuments in Paris. They also can assist you with the purchase of ballet, opera and concert tickets.

➤ Staff at the French tourist offices are exceptionally helpful. They seem truly to want to make your trip special. Of course it's possible you could meet a "sour lemon" but my experiences have been very positive.

TO CONTACT FRENCH GOVERNMENT TOURIST OFFICES

In New York
444 Madison Avenue, 16th Floor
New York, N.Y. 10022
Phone: 212-838-7800

In Chicago
676 North Michigan Avenue Suite, 3360
Chicago, IL 60611
Phone: 312-751-7800

In Los Angeles
9454 Wilshire Boulevard, Suite 715
Beverly Hill, CA 90212
Phone: 310-271-6665

In Paris
127 Avenue des ChampsElysées
01-49-52-53-54

Hotel Selections

Choose a small, preferably Left Bank hotel in the 6th or 7th Arrondissement. (Paris districts are called arrondissements.) These smaller hotels provide personal service and warmth not found in the large, more commercial hotels. Besides my personal suggestions, look through any of the following books, available either at the **Traveler's Bookstore** in New York **(212-664-0995)**, your local bookstore, and of course, on the Internet.

- *Charming Small Hotel Guides* by Rivage (a division of Fodor's).

- *Country Inns of France* by Karen Brown (available at all large bookstores as well as the Traveler's Bookstore).

- *Gault and Milau-Paris* (available at all large bookstores as well as the Traveler's Bookstore).

After deciding on hotels, it is fun to call directly. All the concierges of these hotels speak English. Remember Europe is six hours later. If you phone at 8 a.m. Eastern Standard Time (EST), it is 2 p.m. in Paris. To call a Paris number from the United States, first dial the country code, **011-33**, followed by the city code, which is **1**, and then the number.

You can inquire directly about the prices, facilities and location. The warmth of the owner/manager/concierge will give you a clue about the reception you can expect as well as the services provided. Request a brochure and fax number. The reservation can be confirmed by fax. Some hotels will want a credit card number to hold the room. Others will ask for a one-night deposit to be paid by check. Don't forget to ask what the cancellation policy is regarding your deposit.

TIP: Ask for a quiet room, preferably on the interior garden or courtyard. Ask for a bath, not a shower. The rooms with a bath are larger in size and there is a hand held showerhead in all of the tubs.

TIP: Do not forget to pack a washcloth, because very few hotels in Europe have them.

TIP: All hotels recommended here have outstanding, knowledgeable, English-speaking concierges. They will assist you with restaurant reserva-tions, essentials, shopping sugges-tions, directions, travel arrange-ments — anything and everything including writing in French whatever you need translated. It is like having an adult nanny looking after you.

23

TIP: These hotels are all in outstanding
locations. They are close to great
shopping, museums, major sightseeing, and restaurants in one of
the safest and most elegant neighbor-
hoods in Paris.

TIP: Hotel phone numbers used in *Going
like Lynn* include the country and
city codes.

Call ahead and inquire

about prices and services.

The warmth of the

owner/manager/concierge

will give you

a clue about the reception

you can expect as well

as the services provided.

Personal Favorites

Since currency exchange rates change constantly, prices quoted are approximations using the following rating scale:

1 = reasonable ($70-$100 per night)

2 = moderate ($110-$150 per night)

3 = expensive ($160-$300 per night)

Hôtel Bellechasse (2) 8 Rue Bellechasse Paris 75007. **Metro:** Musée d'Orsay. **Telephone:** 011-33-1-45-50-22-31. **Fax:** 011-33-1- 45-51-52-36. **U.S. Rep.:** CIP 800-949-7562 for reservations. **Rooms:** 43. **Breakfast:** $10. **Location:** right down the street from the d'Orsay Museum, one block from the Bat-o-Bus stop on the Seine (the tourist boat that makes six stops at major tourist sites and runs from May to mid-September. Check for prices and dates with the French tourist bureau or your hotel concierge). Close to the Invalides (Napoleon's Tomb), also to Place de la Concorde. Recently redecorated rooms are fresh and comfortable. It is very hard to get a room so reserve well in advance.

Hôtel Bersoly's (2) 28 Rue de Lille, Paris 75007. **Metro:** Musée d'Orsay. **Telephone:** 011-33-1-42-60-73-79. **Fax:** 011-33-1-49-27-05-55. **Breakfast:** $10. **Credit Cards:** MasterCard, VISA. **Rooms:** 16, tiny but clean and comfortable, with modern bathrooms. **Location:** one block to d'Orsay Museum, one block to the Louvre, one block to the Seine (which divides Paris into the Right Bank and Left Bank). In the midst of antique shops, galleries, boutiques; close to restaurants, cafes and bistros and the best people-watching areas.

Hôtel de La Tulipe (1) 33 Rue Malar, Paris 75007. **Metro:** Latour-Maubourg or Invalides. **Telephone:** 011-33-1- 45-50-67-21; **Fax:** 011-33-1-47-53-96-37. **Location:** An adorable little hotel off of Rue St. Dominique in an ancient convent with wonderful old stone walls. The small rooms are decorated with charming country French fabrics. It is between the Invalides and the Eiffel Tower, near the wonderful food market on Rue de Clec. There are many quaint restaurants and patisseries in the neighborhood.

Hôtel de Nevers (1) 83 Rue du Bac, Paris 75007. **Metro:** Rue du Bac. **Telephone:** 011-33-1-45-55-61-30. **Breakfast:** $6. **Location:** a very small, inexpensive, simple hotel in a great neighborhod, just a few blocks from Boulevard St. Germain. There are two rooms that have a tiny terrace on the top floors with great views. They don't accept credit cards and since there is no elevator, guests must walk up two to four flights.

Hôtel de Varenne (2) 44 Rue de Bourgogne, Paris 75007. **Metro:** Varenne. **Telephone:** 011-33-1-45-51-45-55. **Fax:** 011-33-1-45-41-86-63. **Rooms:** 24. **Breakfast:** $9. **Location:** on a quiet street in the midst of interesting little shops and restaurants. This delightful small hotel is only a five-minute walk from the Rodin Museum and 10 minutes from the d'Orsay Museum. An added feature is the small courtyard garden where you can relax in good weather. The rooms are tiny but warm and homey.

MY FAVORITE PARISIAN HOTEL

Hôtel duc de St. Simon (3)   14 Rue St. Simon, Paris 75007. **Metro:** Rue du Bac. **Telephone:** 011-33-1-45-48-35-66. **Fax:** 011-33-1-45-48-68-25. **Rooms:** 29. **Breakfast:** $15. **Credit Cards:** After 25 years, the St. Simon has finally started accepting all major credit cards. **Location:** on a quiet street, one block from Boulevard St. Germain and Rue du Bac. Near the d'Orsay Museum, Louvre, Rodin Museum, Rue de Grenelle (main Left Bank shopping street), one-half block from Ferme St. Simon, a well-known Parisian restaurant. This intimate hotel is an elegant jewel with exquisite hand-embroidered sheets and towels, and small bedrooms furnished with wonderfully tasteful antiques. Ask for a room overlooking the back garden so you can wake up to birds singing. The bathrooms are modern and luxurious. The small sitting rooms and reception area are filled with fresh flowers. Your breakfast is served on beautiful Limoges china either in your room or in the cellar. Staff is friendly and helpful and the concierges are knowledgeable, as well as gracious. You will fantasize that it is your house. The hardest thing to do at the St. Simon is leave. They even have wash cloths, and you can purchase the Limoges service to take home. Do not forget to ask for the *International Herald Tribune* with your breakfast tray. The hotel staff will assist you in every way to make your stay in Paris special.

29

HÔTEL LENOX (2) 9 Rue de Université, Paris 75007. **Metro:** St.-Germain-des-Prés. **Telephone:** 011-33-1-42-96-10-95. **Fax:** 011-33-1-42-61-52-83. **Rooms:** 32. **Breakfast:** $11. **Location:** in the midst of shopping, art and antique galleries. It is a five minute walk from St.-Germain-des-Prés and ten minutes to the Louvre. Amenities include a charming small bar.

HÔTEL SOLFERINO (1 & 2) 91 Rue de Lille, Paris 75007. **Metro:** Musée d'Orsay. **Telephone:** 011-33-1-47-05-85-54. **Fax:** 011-33-1-45-55-51-16. **Breakfast:** $9. **Location:** one-half block from the d'Orsay Museum and close to Place de la Concorde and Hôtel des Invalides. The staff is helpful and the prices are a great value. The rooms are simple and comfortable. Again, the location is outstanding and the hotel offers simple charm and a friendly staff.

HÔTEL ST. PAUL (2) 14 Rue Monsieur-le-Prince, Paris 75006. **Metro:** Luxembourg. **Telephone:** 011-33-1-47-26-98-64. **Rooms:** 31. **Breakfast:** $10. **Location:** a charming well-run immaculate small hotel near the Panthéon. Bedrooms are freshly decorated and have modern bathrooms. Many rooms have great garden views and small terraces. The cellar is filled with wonderful antiques and flowers. This is the best of the small hotels in this neighborhood, with extremely helpful concierges.

Indulge yourself!

Restaurants

Restaurant phone numbers are given for calling in Paris and include the city code and number, *not the country code*.

Prices, including tip but no wine:

(1) inexpensive ($10-$20)

(2) moderate ($21-$40)

(3) expensive $41 plus.

Those with * are open on Sunday.

FAVORITES IN THE 6TH AND 7TH ARRONDISSEMENTS

Beaux Arts* (1) 11 Rue Bonaparte. **Metro:** St.-Germain-des-Prés. **Telephone:** 01-43-26-92-64. Across the street from the famous art school, École Nationale des Arts. This is one of the biggest bargains in Paris. Typical bistro food such as coq au vin (chicken in wine) or beef stew cooked in wine, is served at long tables filled with students, art dealers and tourists. Great place for local color.

Brasserie Lutetia* (2) Hotel Lutetia, 23 Rue de Sevres. **Metro:** Sevres-Babylone. **Telephone:** 01-49-54-46-76. Open daily until midnight. **Specialties:** veal chops, chicken with thyme, fresh fish (grilled, sautéed or poached).

Chez Marius (3) 5 Rue Bourgogne.
Metro: Solferino. **Telephone:** 01-45-51-79-42.
Good seafood, friendly waiters, close to
Hotel de Varenne.

Ferme St. Simon (3) 6 Rue St. Simon.
Metro: Rue du Bac. **Telephone:** 01-45-48-
35-74. Closed for Saturday lunch and
Sunday. Gracious maitré d and excellent
waiters. Down the street from Hotel St.
Simon and one block from Boulevard
St. Germain and Rue du Bac. Delicious
food. Save room for the homemade
chocolate truffles.

L'affricolé (2 & 3) 47 Rue Malar. **Metro:**
Latour-Maubourg. **Telephone:** 01-44-18-31-
33. Tiny restaurant with delicious food by a
young creative chef who runs into the dining room to see if you like his cuisine.

La Caleche (1) 8 Rue Lille. **Metro:**
Musée d'Orsay. **Telephone:** 01-42-60-24-76.
Next to Hotel Bersoly's. This is a friendly,
small restaurant with very good food.

La Maison de l'Amerique Latine (3)
217 Boulevard St. Germain. **Metro:** Rue du
Bac. **Telephone:** 01-45-49-33-23. In the
Latin American Institute, it is well known
to diplomats and not on the usual tourist
circuit. Closed in August and evenings
October through April, Saturday, Sundays
and holidays. It is a charming 18th century

mansion with a beautiful terrace overlooking a gorgeous garden. Very expensive, delicious cuisine, and fabulous presentation – like dining in a small elegant club. Located right down the street from the Hotel St. Simon. This is a very special restaurant in a charming setting.

La Petite Chaise* **(1 & 2)** 36 Rue de Grenelle. **Metro:** Rue du Bac. **Telephone:** 01-42-22-13-35. A tiny restaurant with elbow-to-elbow tables that is fun and has a warm ambiance.

Le Bellecour (2 & 3) 22 Rue Surcouf; **Metro:** Latour-Maubourg or Invalides. **Telephone:** 01- 45-51-46-93. Small charming restaurant located between the Eiffel Tower and the Invalides (Napoleon's Tomb.) The food is excellent and presentation delightful.

Le Munich* **(2)** 22 Rue G. Apollinaire; (across from Church Saint-Germain-des-Prés). **Metro:** St.-Germain-des-Prés. **Telephone:** 01-47-34-01-06. Lively, crowded Parisian bistro, open daily until 2 a.m. **Specialties:** oysters, calves liver, fresh fish.

Le Petit Laurent (2 & 3) 38 Rue de Varenne. **Metro:** Varenne. **Telephone:** 01-45-48-79-64. Small, charming restaurant with very good food and service.

Polidor (1). 41 Rue Monsieur le Prince.
Metro: Odéon. **Telephone:** 01-43-26-95-34.
Quaint, old bistro with lots of charm and
terrific waitresses. Great Parisian bargain!
Specialties: rabbit in mustard sauce, boeuf
bourguignon, blanquette de veau.

Thomieux* **(1&2)** 79 Rue St. Dominique.
Metro: Invalides. **Telephone:** 01-47-05-49-
75. A wonderful, inexpensive neighborhood
bistro between the Invalides and Eiffel
Tower. Be sure to make reservations since it
is extremely popular with both locals and
tourists. If the pigeon with whole cabbage is
available, it is absolutely delicious. This is
one of the best bargains in Paris. There are
a half-dozen modern, airy hotel rooms
above the restaurant.

Favorites in
Other Neighborhoods

Balzar* (1 & 2) 49 Ecoles (5th arrondissemont). **Metro:** Cluny-La Sorbonne.
Telephone: 01-43-54-13-67. One of the old
left bank brasseries, it is noisy, delicious,
inexpensive and fun! The lamb melts in
your mouth. Tourists and locals have been
coming here for years. Be sure to call for
reservations.

Brasserie Café de la Paix (2 & 3)
Le Grand Hotel 12 Boulevard Capucines
(9th arrondissemont). **Metro:** Opéra.
Telephone: 01-40-07-30-20. Perfect for dinner before or after a performance at the
Opéra Garnier. You can order a grilled fish
here and not worry about the calories.

Coconnos (2&3) 2 bis Place des Vosges
(4th arrondissemont). **Metro:** St.-Paul.
Telephone: 01-42-78-58-16. Closed Monday.
You can eat here for around $30 per person.

Fermette Marbeuf (2&3) 5 Rue
Marbeuf (8th arrondissemont). **Metro:**
Alma- Marceau. **Telephone:** 01-47- 23-31-31.
A wonderful art deco restaurant, convenient
for lunch if you are shopping the Avenue
Montaigne area, and popular with local
business people.

La Dinée (2). 85 Rue Le Blanc (15th arrondissemont). **Not convenient for the Metro so take a taxi**. **Telephone:** 01-45-54-20-49. Closed Saturday and Sunday lunch. Superb young chef, Christian Chabanet, prepares light creative cuisine and presents it beautifully. (I met him when he was the chef at the tiny La Ferronniere in the 7th arrondissement. If you elect to dine alone you will be well received.)

Le Procope (2). 13 Rue Ancienne Comédie (6th arrondissemont). **Metro:** Odéon. **Telephone:** 01-43-26-99-20. One of the oldest restaurants in Paris, it has a charming atmosphere and moderately-priced food. It is well-known and always filled with tourists.

Parisian Bistros
Owned by Famous Chefs

La Rotisserie d'en Face. 2 Rue Christine (6th arrondissemont). **Metro:** Odéon. Chef Jaques Cagna. Closed Saturday lunch and Sunday. **Telephone:** 01-43-26-40-98.

Le Bistro de Cote. 16 Boulevard St. Germain (5th arrondissemont). **Metro:** St.-Germain-des-Prés. Chef Michele Rostang. Closed Saturday lunch and Sunday. **Telephone:** 01-43-54-59-10.

Les Bookinistes. 53 Quai des Grandes Augustins (6th arrondissemont). **Metro:** St.-Michel. Chef Guy Savoy. Closed Saturday lunch and Sunday. **Telephone:** 01-43-25-45-94.

Relais du Parc. 55 Avenue Raymond Poincarre (16th arrondissemont). **Metro:** Victor-Hugo. Started by Chef Joel Robuchon (just retired). Open daily. **Telephone:** 01-44-05-66-10.

Rotisserie de Beaujolais. 19 Quai de la Tournelle (5th arrondissemont), **Metro:** St.-Michel. Chef Claude Terrail. Closed Monday. **Telephone:** 01-43-54-17-47.

Left Bank...
Right Bank...
All around town,
Where to go and what to see!

Where to Go and What to See

LEFT BANK

- **The Invalides**: Napoleon's tomb, army hospital and museum.

- **The Eiffel Tower and Champ des Mars**: Gardens surrounding the tower.

- **Luxembourg Gardens and the Senate**. Wonderful for people watching.

- **Palais Bourbon**: The French congress, called the Assemblé Nationale.

- **Saint-Germaine-des-Prés**: The church and neighborhood of antique shops, book sellers, galleries, boutiques, cafés and restaurants.

- **Rue de Seine, Rue Bonaparte**: Principal streets for left bank art galleries.

- **Rue de Grenelle, Rue de Dragon, Rue de Rennes**: Well-known designer boutiques line these narrow streets.

- **Rue de Buci, Rue de Cler, Rue Mouffetard**: Filled with food markets, restaurants and carry-out — a veritable feast.

- **Panthéon**: Tombs of French notables

- **The Botanical Gardens**: Acres of beautiful plants and flowers.

- **Place Von Furstenberg**: An exquisite historic square near St.-Germain-des-Prés. Today's inabitants are slick fabric shops, decorator studios and a small museum.

RIGHT BANK

- **Champs-Elysées**: Major boulevard, with the Arc de Triomphe at one end and Place de la Concorde at the other.

- **Place de la Concorde**: The historic square with Egyptian obelisk. For me, this is the center of Paris. The views are breathtaking.

- **Opéra Garnier**: Opera house fit for kings with enough gilt to light up the city.

- **Opéra Bastille**: The modern opera house near the ancient prison.

- **The Tuileries**: Gardens between the Louvre and l'Orangerie museums.

- **Place Vendome**: Elegant square that is home to the famous Ritz Hotel and the world's most expensive jewelers.

- **Saint Eustache**: Gothic church in the old Les Halles district (original farmer's market).

- **Montmartre**: 19th century artists' quarter with Sacre Coeur Church at the top, offering stunning views of Paris.

- **The Marais**: This ancient swamp has been converted into an avant garde neighborhood with boutiques, galleries and lovely 17th century mansions that today are museums and government buildings.

- **Place des Vosges**: Beautiful square in the middle of the Marais district. This is the oldest square in Paris.

- **Trocadéro**: Museum and theatre complex across from the Eiffel Tower.

- **Avenue Montaigne**: Street of shops for couture clothes, elegant linens and accessories.

- **Avenue Gabriel**: Home of the French President–the Elysée Palace and gardens are here.

- **Fauchon's and Hediards:**: The world's fanciest grocery stores near the Madeleine church.

ISLANDS & BRIDGES

Ile de la Cité
- **Notre-Dame and Church Gardens:** The Michelin Guide describes this gothic cathedral in the middle of the Seine as "one of the supreme masterpieces of French art."

- **Sainte-Chapelle:** One of the loveliest small churches in Paris. The stained glass windows are magical.

- **Conciergerie:** An ancient prison where Marie Antoinette and other nobles were held during the revolution. From La Conciergerie, many were taken to the guillotine to be beheaded.

- **Palais de Justice:** The French courts (interior closed to the public).

- **The Flower Market:** A great place to buy yourself an inexpensive bouquet (open mornings only).

Ile St-Louis
- The Quais (river banks)
- Four blocks of 18th century apartments overlooking the Seine. Charming boutiques, galleries and the famous, expensive ice cream café–Berthillon.

Special Bridges
- Pont Neuf
- Pont Alexandre
- Pont de la Concorde

Paris Museums: Personal Favorites

In the U.S.: *You can order a museum pass 3–4 weeks before your trip from* **H.S.A. VOYAGE** - 1-800-927-4765 or 817-483-9400.

In Paris: *Passes are available at the French Tourist Office or at the Museums.*

- **Musée Cluny:** 6 Place Paul Painlené. 5th arrondissement. **Metro**: Cluny. **Telephone**: 01-43-25-62-00. **Hours**: 9:15 a.m–5:45 p.m. Closed Tuesdays. Superb medieval collection of sculptures, tapestries and paintings in ancient Gallo-Roman baths.

- **Musée Nissim de Camondo:** 63 Rue Monceau Paris 8th arrondissement. **Metro**: Villiers. **Telephone**: 01-45-63-26-32. **Hours**: 10 a.m. – 12 p.m.; 2–5 p.m. Closed Mondays and Tuesdays. Outstanding private collection of 18th century furniture and decorative arts in a 19th century mansion.

- **Musée de l'Orangerie.** Place de la Concorde 1st arrondissement. **Metro**: Concorde. **Telephone**: 01-42-97-48-16. **Hours**: 9:45 a.m. – 5:15 p.m. Closed Tuesdays. A lovely collection of Impressionist art with two rooms of Monet's water lilies.

- **Musée Marmottan.** 2 Rue Louis Boilly. 16th arrondissement. **Metro**: La Muette. **Telephone:** 01-42-24-07-02. **Hours**: 10 a.m.– 5 p.m. Closed Mondays. Impressionist paintings in a splendid mansion. Includes outstanding Monets on the lower level.

- **Musée Picasso.** Hôtel Sale, 5 Rue de Thorigny, 3rd arrondissement. **Metro**: St. Paul. **Telephone**: 01-42-71-25-21. **Hours**: 9 a.m.– 6 p.m. April through September,

9:30 a.m.– 5:30 p.m. January through March. Closed Tuesdays. A 17th century private residence restored to house Picasso's art, collection of contemporary art, and personal photos and letters.

- **Musée Rodin:** 77 Rue Varenne, 7th arrondissement, **Metro**: Varenne. **Telephone**: 01-44-18-61-10. **Hours**: 9:30 a.m.– 4:45 p.m. Closed Mondays. Rodin's large sculptures are in the gardens, and smaller pieces are inside, along with his collection of contemporary art and photography.

- **Musée Zadkine:** 100 Bis Rue d'Assas, 6th arrondissement. **Metro:** Port-Royal. **Telephone:** 01-43-26-91-90. **Hours:** 10 a.m.–5:40 p.m. Closed Mondays. The original studios of sculptor Zadkine. More than 100 of his works are on display.

- **Musée Maillol:** 61 rue de Grenelle Paris 7th, **Metro:** Rue du Bac. **Telephone:** 01-42-22-59-58. **Hours:** 11 a.m.– 6 p.m. Closed Tuesdays. The newest private museum to open in Paris. The 18th century building has been renovated for Maillol's monu-mental sculptures, as well as works by other 20th century artists.

- **Musée d'Orsay:** 1 Rue de Bellechase, 7th arrondissement. **Metro:** Musée d'Orsay. **Telephone:** 01-40-49-48-14. **Hours:** Tuesday, Wednesday, Friday, Saturday, 10 a.m.– 6 p.m. Thursday 10 a.m.– 9:45 p.m. Sunday 9 a.m.–6 p.m. Closed Mondays. The old Paris railroad station has been converted into a modern muse-um. It is home to one of the world's most significant collections of Impressionist art, and a permanent exhibit of art-noveau furniture and decorative arts. Have lunch on the second level.

The Best Shopping Areas

- Shop **Rue de Grenelle** from Rue du Bac to Rue des Rennes to Boulevard St. Germain for well known French and Italian designers. You will also see many designer boutiques that are not well known in America. Be sure to check out Robert Merloz, Chacok, Paul Ka as well as Claude Montana, Sonia Rykiel, Issey Miyake and Tehen.

- For younger, more avant-garde fashions, do not miss the **Marais District** (3rd and 4th arrondissements). From the Place des Vosges to the Picasso Museum you will pass dozens of small boutiques. Popy Moreni is one of the most interesting.

- The super haute couture shops with super high prices are located in the **8th arrondissement**. Walk down Avenue Montaigne, Rue François Premier and

Avenue George V. A few names you will see: Christian Dior, Nina Ricci, Jean Louis Scherrer, Balmain, Givenchy, Yves St. Laurent and Jill Sanders.

- In the 2nd arrondissement, across from the Ritz Hotel, the **Place des Victoires** and around the corner, Rue Etienne Marcel. Here you can find Kenzo's original boutique along with Thierry Mugler, Dorothy Bis, Comme des Garcons and Claude Barthlemy. Mendes, the big discount shop for French designers, is a block away at 65 Rue Montmartre.

GREAT PURCHASES

- Museum shops have charming gifts from postcards and notepads to books, posters and copies of small objects of art.

PERFUMES

- Duty free perfume shops on Rue de Rivoli, and upscale perfume shops on Rue Royal.

- Airport boutiques and non-stop flights from Paris to the U.S. all sell duty-free perfume.

- For special unique scents, shop **Patricia de Nicolaï** at 80 Rue de Grenelle, 7th arrondissement. Open 10 a.m.– 2 p.m. and 3 – 7 p.m. The shop is owned by Guerlain's granddaughter. Besides perfumes, she sells candles, potpourris and crystal perfume flacons — fabulous gifts!

47

CHOCOLATES

*How about handmade dark chocolates
packed beautifully in tiny sacs or lovely little
boxes? Everyone has a favorite chocolatier.
You should try:*

- **Debauve and Gallais** for dark chocolate
  covered orange slices, 30 Rue St. Peres
  (7th arrondissement). Open 10 a.m.–
  7 p.m. Closed Sundays.

- **Dalloyou** on Rue de Grenelle at Rue du
  Bac (7th arrondissement) for chocolate
  truffles.

- **Christian Constant**: 26 Rue du Bac (7th
  arrondissement). Open daily 8 a.m.–8 p.m

- **Lenôtre**: 44 Rue du Bac (7th arrondissement), open daily 9 a.m.–9 p.m. Sundays
  until 1 p.m.

- **La Maison du Chocolat**: 225 Rue
  du Fauboug St. Honore (8th arrondissement). Open 9:30 a.m.–7 p.m. Closed
  Sundays.

SMOKED SALMON

- **Petrossian**: 18 Boulevard de Latour
  Maubourg (7th arrondissement). Open
  9 a.m.–8 p.m. Closed Sundays. Petrossian
  salmon is sliced paper thin and sealed in
  airtight packages.

- **Comptoir du Saumon**: 61 Rue Pierre
  Charron (8th arrondissement). Good
  assortment and good prices.

- All food markets and small delicatessens
  (traiteurs) will cut you a few slices–great
  snack for your return flight. For me, I'd
  sell my soul for just a few slices with
  those wonderful mini blinis. It's an
  extravagance not to be missed!

SCARVES

*Every designer boutique sells its own signature
scarf. Prices range from around $100–$250
for a pure silk designer scarf. They also are
available at airport boutiques. Synthetic copies
are sold in lower end department stores like*
Monoprix, *in small shops on Rue de Rivoli
and from outdoor venders for around $5 to $10.*

HOME ACCENTS

- **Un Air de Giverny**. 10 Rue de Bellechase
  (7th arrondissement). Open 11 a.m.–6 p.m.
  Closed Sundays and Mondays. Monet's
  blue and yellow china, place mats, nap-
  kins and a lovely assortment of small
  decorative objects make wonderful gifts.
  The store is across the street from the
  d'Orsay Museum.

LIPSTICKS

*Great selection at all cosmetic counters.
(Best prices at **Monoprix**.)*

LINGERIE

- **Seraphina**: 22 Rue du Vieux Colombier
  (6th arrondissement). **Telephone:** 01-45-
  48-16-62. Fabulous selection of little lace
  underwear in a tiny tiny boutique.
  Moderate to expensive.

- **Monoprix**: Rue de Rennes at Boulevard
  St. Germain. This Monoprix has great
  inexpensive copies of bras and panties in
  contemporary colors.

FLOWERS

- **Rose Theatre**: 22 Rue de Bellechase.
  Telephone: 01-45-51-41-41, down the street
  from the d'Orsay Museum. The young
  florists are talented artists. It's breathtaking
  to just walk into the shop and look.

49

UNUSUAL SILKS

- **Compagnie Francaise de l'Orient, et de la Chine**: 260 Boulevard. St. Germain (7th arrondissement). **Telephone:** 01-47-05-92-82. Interesting affordable silk coordinates, not sold in the U. S. A two piece silk outfit runs about $350. The clothes are understated and well made.

ANTIQUES

- **Shop Rue St. Peres**. Rue de Beaune and Rue de Lille in the 7th arrondissement.

- **Village Saint-Paul.** 23–27 Rue St. Paul in the 4th arrondissement is a delightful place to browse. Closed Tuesdays and Wednesdays.

- **Marais District**. There are over 70 dealers. Shop the small antique shops on the side streets off Place des Vosges.

- **Le Marché aux Puces**, the world's largest antique market. Open Friday morning through Monday afternoon. Watch your valuables. Pickpockets prey on tourists.

GENERAL SHOPPING

- **The Monoprix** on Rue de Rennes at Boulevard St. Germain is like our Kmart or Target.

- **Airport Duty Free Shops** have wonderful salmon, cheeses, caviar and pates. All make great gifts or lunch for the flight home.

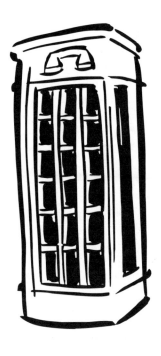

Carry an international telephone card
like AT&T Direct, MCI, Sprint
or other similar international service.

Post offices in France
also will make international calls for you.

French Essentials

- **Directions:** Always have a city and metro map and card of your hotel with you. On foot: Ask a police officer, hotel doorman or passersby. Show your map and write out where you want to go. On bus, Metro or taxi: Write out where you want to go — name, street address, arrondissement, and between what major streets. Ask the concierge for help before you take the Metro, bus or taxi.

- **Toilettes:** Où sont les toilettes s'il vous plaît? Where is the toilet? Located in cafés, department stores, large hotels, theatres, museums, monuments and train stations. The flusher in France is often on the floor, on the wall, or on a chain — you must search for it! A small tip is expected in dish on sink (2-3 francs).

- **Light Switches:** Located in hallways. Sometimes the public toilets and hallways are on two-minute timers. Press timer again, if they suddenly go out.

- **Money Exchange:** American Express office or ask Concierge for nearest bank that changes currency. It is cheaper to change two or three traveler's checks than one at a time.

- **Automated Teller Machines (ATMs):**
  Call your bank and make sure your card
  is properly coded for international trans-
  actions. ATMs in France are as conve-
  niently located as they are in large U.S.
  cities. Please use an ATM only in the
  daytime and with attention to safety
  and security.

- **Telephone:** Have an international
  telephone card like AT&T Direct, MCI,
  Sprint or other similar international services. Check with your long distance car-
  rier before leaving. Post offices in France
  also will make international calls for you.
  Direct dial is available from most hotels.
  Check with your concierge.

ADDITIONAL RESOURCES

- **Green Michelin Guide – Paris**
  (complete sightseeing information).

- **Fodor's – Paris** (general guide book).

- **Frommer's – Paris** (general guide book).

- **Travel & Leisure–Paris** (my personal
  choice, published by Macmillan Travel.)

- **Food Lovers Guide to Paris** by Patricia
  Wells (an American authority on French
  cuisine).

- **Gault and Milau Paris** (French author-
  ities on French cuisine).

- **Born to Shop Paris** by Sally Gershman.

- Magazines and newspaper articles.

- Suggestions from friends and travel
  agents.

TIPPING

PARIS HOTELS

- **S.C.** means Service Compris in hotels or restaurants where the service is included. However, you can give a little extra for great service.

- **Concierge:** Tip is expected. $3 to $10 per day, if you receive great help.

- **Room Service:** Tip is optional. If you have breakfast in your room or in the breakfast room, $1 left on the tray or a 5 franc piece.

- **Maid:** Tip is optional. $1 to $2 (5 to 10 francs) a day, depending on the hotel or if a special service is rendered, such as providing extra hangers or pillows.

- **Porter:** Tip is expected. $2 (10 francs) when checking in and again at check out.

- **Special Services:** Tip is expected when ordering a vase, bottled water, glasses, etc. to be delivered to your room.

COUNTRYSIDE HOTELS AND INNS

- **Concierge:** If concierge is owner, no tipping. If not, $2 to $4 a day for extra service only.

- **Maid:** Tip is optional — $1 per day.

- **Waiter:** Tip is optional — Leave about $2 per meal.

- **Maitre'd:** In small hotel, tip is optional. $2 a day if he helped you with menu or wine selection, or was especially courteous and friendly.

RESTAURANTS

- **S.C. – Service Compris:** Service is included so 15 percent is automatically added to your bill, but leave small extra change. In fancy restaurants, if your bill is more than 200 francs and the maitre'd gave you great assistance, you can give him an optional 20 francs plus 20 francs left on the table for the waiter.

- **Service Non Compris (not included):** leave a straight 15 percent tip.

- **Coat Check:** 5 to 10 francs depending on how fancy the restaurant.

- **Taxis:** Tip 10 percent of the total fare.

Safety

- Check valuables, passport, traveler's checks, credit cards and cash in hotel safe.

- Keep four $5 bills and five $1 bills with you. Keep 200 to 300 francs ($40 to $60) with you.

- Keep a credit card (you should travel with two: MasterCard, VISA and/or American Express) so if one is lost or stolen you have another working card. Keep cards in separate places.

- When you change money, you will need your passport. Otherwise, leave your passport in the hotel safe!!!

- Take the Metro only during daylight hours.

- Wear a money belt, fanny pack, or small shoulder bag across your shoulder with the opening turned towards your body.

- Do not wear jeans, shorts or white sneakers — they are American tourist symbols. It is like advertising to thieves that you are an easy mark.

- If for any reason you feel uncomfortable, get off the street and find a cafe or tabac (they are everywhere). Ask them to call a taxi, showing card of your hotel. Say: "Appelez-moi un taxi s'il vous plait." Offer 4 or 5 francs for the call and hold out money in your hand.

A tiny box of chocolates
is like buying a small tin of caviar.
They are usually hand made and very, very
expensive, but oh so delicious.
Great present!

French Prizes and Surprises

- Wine and coffee are cheaper than Coke, scotch and tea.

- Hotel breakfasts are double the price of a small cafe.

- A tiny box of chocolates is like buying a small tin of caviar. They are usually hand made and very, very expensive, but oh so delicious. Great present!

- An inexpensive Parisian diet lunch in a cafe is 30 to 40 francs ($6 to $12). Try Salade Composée — usually salad greens with either ham or real chicken and vinaigrette dressing or Salade Niçoise — salad greens with canned tuna, black olives, tiny potatoes and vinaigrette dressing.

- Museums and cafés are another great place for inexpensive to moderate lunches.

- All restaurants post menus outside with prices. Le Menu or Plat du Jour is a special price and usually a very good value.

- Remember S.C. = service included and B.C. = boisson (beverage) included.

- The menu usually consists of three courses: appetizer, main course and dessert. A la carte is generally more expensive.

- Degustation on the menu is from a grand restaurant and it is the chef's special sampling of specialties. It is too much food and too rich for most American stomachs.

- Hotel breakfasts are coffee, tea or chocolate with French bread, croissant, jams and butter and sometimes orange juice. Eggs, fruit, etc. are all extra and very expensive.

- Mineral water, snacks and fruit are cheaper to buy at the corner grocery than the hotel, and it is a lot more fun.

- French lingerie: You will pass lots of tiny boutiques. They are expensive but worth it. Lingerie is gorgeous and fun to buy in Paris.

Important Paris Telephone Numbers

U.S. Embassy: 01-42-96-12-02
2 Avenue Gabriel

Tourist Information:
01-49-52-53-54
(for recorded information)

French Government Tourist Office:
01-49-52-53-54
127 Avenue des Champs Elysees

Doctors (SOS):
01-47-07-77-77
24-Hour House Calls

24-Hour Ambulance (SAMU):
Dial 15

Lost or Stolen Credit Cards:
01-42-77-11-90

Cultural Review in English:
01-49-52-53-56

Renting a
chauffeur-driven car with an
English-speaking driver is an
excellent way to see the sights
in a short period of time.

How to See Paris—Suggested Itineraries

A Two-Day Overview

DAY ONE

My first suggestion is to rent a chauffeur-driven car with an English-speaking driver for 3-1/2 to 4 hours. It will cost approximately $150.

➤ Start by driving up to Montmartre (the old artists quarter, high on a hilltop overlooking Paris).

➤ Pass the Louvre with the Tuileries Gardens on your left.

➤ Next, pass Palais Royal and Bibliotheque Nationale, driving north up Avenue de l'Opéra. Take a mini detour to Place Vendome, a beautiful and historic square, home to the Ritz Hotel and some of the world's most fabulous jewelers. Past Place Vendôme, on your left is the magnificently restored Paris opera house, Opéra Garnier.

➤ Get out at Sacré-Coeur, the huge cathedral on top of the hill, and enjoy the fabulous view of Paris. Visit the interior of Sacré-Coeur and take a brief walk around Place du Tertre.

➤ After Montmartre, ask your driver to pass by Fauchons and Hediards, two of the world's most elite grocery stores. They are right before the Madeleine Church at Faubourg St. Honore. Next turn right passing the the Elysée Palace and then over to the Rond Point and up the Champs-Elysées to the Arc de Triomphe. Park on a side street and get out and enjoy the view back to the Place de la Concorde. This is another picture perfect postcard of Paris.

➤ Next, drive back down the Champs-Elysées, turning right on Avenue Montaigne. On both sides of the street are the couture houses of Paris (Dior, Ricci, Jean Louis, Scherrer, etc.) The ready-to-wear is on the main or first floors, where you will find outfits for $1,500 to $2,000. Upstairs is the custom made department, with prices starting around $20,000. You will also find perfume and accessories for $30 to $50.

➤ Continue on to the Trocadero. You are now directly across the river from the Eiffel Tower, another fabulous view.

➤ Cross the Seine to the Left Bank and stop for a quick photo at the Eiffel Tower.

➤ Driving on the quai of the Left Bank of the Seine, you will have another spectacular view from the gardens in front of the Invalides (Napoleon's Tomb.) On your right are the magnificent grounds of the Invalides and across the river are the Grand Palais and Petit Palais with the beautiful Alexandre Bridge in between.

➤ Right after the Invalides is the Palais Bourbon, which today is the French Assembly, like our congress. Now you are directly across from the Place de la Concorde with the exquisite view of the Obelisk and the Madeleine Church behind it. I never tire of this view of Paris, particularly from the middle of the bridge. You can come back tomorrow on foot.

➤ Your driver will continue on Boulevard St. Germain past St.-Germain-des-Prés to Luxembourg Gardens. The palace here is the French Senate.

➤ Next, you will have a quick view of the Panthéon before you pass Sorbonne University.

➤ The driver will take you across the Seine to the island in the middle called Ile de la Cité. Here are the courts, the flower market, St.-Chapelle Church, and one of the major sights of Paris, Notre-Dame

Cathedral. Then go over the small bridge to the smallest island, Ile St. Louis with its lovely 18th century apartment buildings surrounded by the Seine.

➤ From Ile St.-Louis, you will cross back to the Right Bank, continuing on to the Marais District, stopping at the Place des Vosges, one of the oldest districts in Paris. Here you will find avant-garde boutiques, galleries, antique shops, restaurants and fabulous old mansions that today are used as government buildings and museums. This is a good stopping place for your four-hour sightseeing trip.

➤ Choose a restaurant and enjoy a relaxing lunch or snack.

➤ After lunch, I recommend walking the Marais District and visiting the Picasso Museum, where you will enjoy viewing the interior of one of the grand old mansions.

➤ Take a taxi back to you hotel and stop for a coffee or drink at one of your neighborhood outdoor cafes.

➤ After dinner, if you still have energy, take a boat tour up and down the Seine on Les Bateaux-Mouches to see Paris illuminated at night. It is a glorious sight and a great way to end your first day in Paris.

DAY TWO

*At breakfast, decide where you want
to spend your time in Paris after your
overview driving tour. You can go shopping,
sightseeing, antiquing, gallery hopping, to
museums or street markets. If you can't
decide, here are a few more suggestions:*

➤ **9:30 a.m.** Start by walking to the Louvre.
Enter with your pass at the Richelieu
Gates and ask at the information desk for
directions to Napoleon's Apartments.

➤ **10:30 a.m.** Leave the Louvre and walk
through the Tuileries Gardens, stopping
briefly at a kiosk for a coffee.

➤ **11:00 a.m.** Visit the top floor of the
d'Orsay Museum where you will find
the Impressionist Collection. Also enjoy
the gorgeous views of Paris from windows or terrace if weather permits.

➤ **12:15 p.m.** Have lunch in the gilt dining
room on the second level of the d'Orsay.

➤ **1:45 p.m.** Walk down the quai to Rue
Bonaparte. Enjoy the galleries and turn
left at Rue Jacob, where you will find
more galleries, antique shops and boutiques. At Rue de Furstenberg, turn right
and walk to the beautiful square surrounded by elegant decorator and textile

studios and the tiny Delacroix Museum, which was the artist's studio in the mid-19th century. Return to Rue Jacob, turn right until Rue de Seine. Turn right again until Rue de Buci and then turn left. You are now in one of the old Parisien street markets. Stop for a crepe and coffee. Exit Rue de Buci at the corner. Turn right at Rue Mazarine and walk a block or so until the Rue de l'Ancienne Comedie, a 17th century street where the 1686 Café Procope still exists.

➢ **3:30 p.m.** Walk back down Boulevard St. Germaine to Rue de Rennes. Turn left and stop at Monoprix to buy small gifts. Downstairs are cosmetics, lingerie and food.

➢ **4:15 p.m.** Turn right when you leave Monoprix, at Rue de Grenelle. Turn right again. Here are all the fancy boutiques. Wander the street until Rue St. Peres. Turn right and cross Boulevard St. Germain. On the left side is the fabulous chocolate shop, Debauve and Gallois. Buy some sinful truffles and dark chocolate covered orange and ginger strips. I am practically salivating just thinking about them.

➤ Before returning to your hotel, go back to Boulevard St. Germain and have a drink at Café des Flores or Deux Magots—both landmark Parisian cafes.

➤ Tonight, enjoy a performance of ballet, opera or music at the Opéra Garnier or Opéra Bastille. Another choice would be a chamber group at one of the small churches followed by a late, light supper. Of course, you could just enjoy a delicious leisurely dinner and plan your next, much longer, visit to Paris.

Keep alcohol and coffee
intake modest on your first day.
Jet lag, rich foods
and alcohol do not mix well.

An Example of a Perfect One-Week Trip

DAY ONE

➤ Fly to Paris on Saturday evening. Most flights arrive between 8 and 11 a.m. Take a taxi to the hotel or pre-arrange with the hotel or travel agent to have a car service meet you. Hand the driver a card with the name, street address, arrondissement (zip code) and between what boulevards or well-known streets, or use the hotel brochure (it usually has a map on the back). Drop your bags (normally hotel rooms are not ready in Europe before noon). Use the hotel powder room to freshen up, brush your teeth and change your blouse or shoes. Do whatever makes you feel rejuvenated after a seven to eight hour flight. Take your map and stroll your new neighborhood.

➤ Between noon and 1 p.m., find a little cafe to sit down and order a light lunch. Examples: omelet, salad, mineral water; Salade-Niçoise: lettuce and cold potatoes, tuna and olives; Salade-Poulet: lettuce, cold chicken; bowl of onion soup, salad; Steak Pomme Frites: small grilled steak, French fries; poached or grilled fish fillet.

➤ Continue your leisurely stroll. Return
to the hotel between 3 and 4 p.m. and
unpack. Sleep for three hours. Have
concierge make dinner reservations
nearby for 8 p.m. and wake you at
7 p.m. Relax in tub or shower. Dress
for dinner. Walk to the restaurant.

➤ Ask maître'd or waiter for help with dinner and wine selection. You can order a
glass of wine, $\frac{1}{2}$ bottle, or $\frac{1}{4}$ carafe in
most places. Mineral water, either natur-
al or with gas, is also usually available
in a $\frac{1}{2}$ bottle. It is expensive, but worth
it. No worries about getting "traveler's
stomach" from unfamiliar water. Order
something simple.

➤ Enjoy your dinner, the food, the presentation, and the people watching, and
learning about a delightful new cuisine.
Feel free to ask the waiters questions
about the wonderful plates going by. Pay
your bill with either French francs or a
credit card. In a good restaurant, the bill
will be between 150 and 250 francs. The
tip is included, but you can leave extra
change (5 to 10 francs). Ask for a card or
matches as a souvenir.

➤ Take a stroll for a block or two and sit
down at a cafe to watch the local scene.
Order coffee or mineral water and praise
yourself for a successful, enjoyable day.

DAY TWO

➣ *7:30–9 a.m.:* Dress and enjoy a continental breakfast either in your room or
in the Breakfast Room. Continental is a
choice of very strong coffee (black or
with milk), tea (with milk or lemon), or
hot chocolate, accompanied by croissant,
thick slices of French bread, with butter
and jams. Sometimes juice is also included. Be sure to wear comfortable walking
shoes, but no sneakers. (They label you
as an American tourist.) Wear solid
trousers or skirts with a tailored jacket,
solid blouse or suit. Leave your wild
prints and large bright patterned clothes
at home. Basics work best. (Try adding a
silk scarf like the French women wear.)
Do not forget to take your raincoat.
Check your tote bag. Be sure to carry:

- Hotel card or brochure.

- Paris map and green Michelin
  Guidebook.

- If you take photos, use a lightweight
  or disposable camera. Do not forget
  the film.

- Your small purse or fanny pack
  should hold 300 francs, a credit card,
  $25 American dollars, your pocket
  notebook (with all of your information and addresses) and another
  hotel card.

➤ Before leaving the hotel, ask the concierge to make a dinner reservation for you for 8 p.m.

➤ **9:15 a.m.–noon.** Leave for your $2\frac{1}{2}$ hour Paris tour by mini-bus or tour bus.

➤ **12:30–2:45 p.m.** Have lunch and visit Louvre Museum. Enter at Richelieu entrance. Café is downstairs. At lunch, study the Louvre Plan and decide what is most important for you to visit. The Louvre is so vast that it takes at least 25 minutes to walk to the gallery where Mona Lisa is located. Then there are long lines and the painting is now behind a plexiglas wall. Personally, I would go back at night when it is less busy and just go see the new galleries like Napoleon's Apartments and the medieval sculpture or the superb new Egyptian Wing. They are fascinating, less crowded and easy to reach.

➤ **2:45–3:15 p.m.** Walk through the Tuileries Gardens. It is the park adjacent to the Louvre. Take a break and have a coffee or cold drink at one of the little stands. Enjoy watching this typical Parisian scene—babies, matrons, dogs, students and older adults—all taking in the air.

➤ *3:30–4:30 p.m.* Visit the Orangerie Museum at the other end of Tuileries. The Impressionist collection is outstanding. The lower level is a fabulous room of Monet's Water Lilies.

➤ *4:30–5:15 p.m.* Walk back to your hotel, crossing the bridge at Pont de la Concorde. Stop and enjoy the view from the bridge. You will pass the National Assembly, then follow the Seine and watch the boat traffic go by. Continue your walk past the d'Orsay Museum. (It is a converted train station and covers a whole city block.)

➤ *5:15–5:45 p.m.* Stop at the cafe at the corner of Quai Anatole France and Rue de Bac. Have a Kir (white wine and creme de cassis). It is delicious and refreshing!

➤ *5:45–6:30 p.m.* Visit a lingerie boutique, a chocolate shop or any of the stunning antique shops on Rue du Bac. (French bras are gorgeous!)

➤ *6:40 p.m.* Return to your hotel and dress for dinner. Wear a simple suit, dress or trouser outfit, nice pumps and a small purse well accessorized with pearls or a pin. You are in Paris and women still look terrific. They have that understated chic that is truly elegant.

➤ *8:00 p.m.* Walk to the restaurant Ferme St. Simon. Enjoy a leisurely delicious dinner with wine. Do not hesitate to ask assistance with ordering from the maitre'd. (They also have menus in funny misspelled English.) Save some calories for the home made chocolate truffles served after dinner with your dessert. They are pure ambrosia and truly sinful!

➤ **After Dinner:** Stroll back to your hotel. Sweet dreams!

DAY THREE

➤ *8:00 a.m. Bonjour. Petit Déjeuner s'il vous plait. Cafe au lait complet.* (Good morning. Coffee with milk complete with bread and jams.)

➤ *9:30–11 a.m.* Walk to the d'Orsay Museum. Visit the top floor Impressionist collection. Also walk out on the terrace for a fabulous view of Paris.

➤ *11:00 a.m.–12:45 p.m.* Walk past the Invalides to Rue de Varennes to the Rodin Museum. Enjoy a coffee or tea in the garden while viewing the fabulous sculpture.

➤ *12:45–2:15 p.m.* Exit museum.
Turn right onto Rue to Varennes. Turn
left on Rue de Bourgogne. Turn right
on Rue de Grenelle. Cross Boulevard
Raspail. Go one block or so and you will
see Restaurant La Chaise. This is a very
typical inexpensive Parisian lunch spot
for locals who work or live in this area.
(Inexpensive lunch is three courses under
$16 - service and beverage included.)

➤ *2:15–3:45 p.m.* Continue walking and
shopping on Rue de Grenelle. It is one of
the best shopping streets with every boutique that you have ever heard of. Turn
left at Rue de Rennes. Go into Monoprix,
an inexpensive department store.
Lingerie and cosmetics are downstairs.
Lipsticks are great gifts!

➤ *3:45–5:00 p.m.* Visit church of St.-
Germain-des-Prés on the corner of
Boulevard St. Germain and Rue des
Rennes. Continue right down Boulevard
St. Germain. Turn left on Rue Mabillon.
Walk until Rue de Buci (a great street
market). Walk back down Rue de
Université. Watch for Place Von
Furstenberg—a beautiful square with
decorator shops and a small museum
of Delacroix.

➤ **5:00 – 6:00 p.m.** Return to Boulevard St. Germain and turn right on Rue de Seine. You will pass wonderful art galleries. At the Seine, turn left. Wander through the bookstalls. Buy a few souvenir photos, postcards or drawings. Turn left at Rue des St. Pères. Stop and buy a small box of chocolates at Debauvier and Gallien Chocolatier.

➤ **6:15 p.m**. Stop at Les Deux Magots at the corner of St. Peres and Boulevard St. Germain for a snack and drink. Example: ham and cheese sandwich, salad or bowl of soup. (It is an over-priced, well-known tourist café, but fun to see once.)

➤ **7:00 p.m.** After returning to your hotel, order a taxi for 7:30 p.m. Leave for concert, opera or ballet performance.

➤ **10:30 p.m.** After the performance, choose a cafe or restaurant nearby and have a late light supper or desert.

➤ **11:30 p.m.** Take a taxi home. Show card of hotel. Tip 10 percent. If there is no cab stand on the street, ask someone at the cafe to call a taxi.

➤ **Midnight.** Bonne Nuit!

DAY FOUR

➢ **_Morning._** Sightseeing. Walk to quai in front of the d'Orsay Museum. Buy a ticket for Bat-O-Bus for Notre Dame. (It is a boat taxi on the Seine River and only runs from May through September. Check the exact dates with your concierge.) Disembark and visit Notre Dame Cathedral. After Notre Dame cross the little bridge to Ile St. Louis. Walk around this tiny, charming island in the middle of the Seine. Stop for refreshments at a café (indoor or outdoor depending on the weather) or have an ice creme at the very chic, very expensive Berthillion (42 Rue St. Louis en L'ile). Take a taxi to Place des Vosges, a beautiful square in one of the oldest districts of Paris — the Marais.

➢ Have lunch at Place des Vosges at any cafe where you like the menu. (Remember: Menus are posted outside all restaurants.) Exit Place des Vosges and follow map and signs to the Picasso Museum in Hotel Salé. In route to the Picasso Museum, you can visit the Carnavalet Museum in adjoining historic mansions that today house a collection illustrating the history of Paris.

➢ Enjoy the wonderful Picasso Museum.
Modern art is displayed in an 18th
Century mansion. It is a truly fabulous
building and collection. Walk to the
Pompidou Centre if you have any feet
left. If not, take a taxi.

➢ Pompidou Centre is the controversial
modern art museum opened in the
1970s. The structure looks like unfin-
ished scaffolding. If you like 20th
Century art, both European and
American, this is a must. Outside the
street life is alive with mimes and acro-
bats. It is always crowded and colorful.
Beware of pickpockets!

➢ After your Pompidou exploration, you
should definitely be ready for a taxi back
to the hotel. Unwind with a glass of wine
and soak your feet in the tub. If you are
exhausted and do not feel like a big dinner, walk to the corner café or brasserie,
for an omelet, salad or soup. Turn in
early. Write in your journal and catch
up with your postcards to family, friends
and coworkers.

DAY FIVE

➢ Take the morning train to Fontainbleau (about a half-hour trip). Check with the concierge for station and schedule. Visit the chateau and gardens, then find a taxi to take you to Barbizon (about a 15 minute ride). It is a little village on the other side of Fontainbleau Forest, where the Barbizon painters lived in the late 19th Century. The town looks like time passed it by. Nothing has changed. Before you leave in the morning, have your concierge book a table for lunch at Bas Breau, an 18th Century poste house that is today an elegant country inn and restaurant popular with Parisians on weekends. (Expensive, but worth it because the food and atmosphere are superb!)

➢ After lunch, wander the little street. Then take a taxi back to Fontainebleau for your return trip to Paris. Be sure to check the schedule so you know exactly what time the train runs.

➢ Tonight, book a cruise, Paris Illumunin- ation for 8:30 p.m. or a nightclub show in Montmartre. Check with your concierge for tour options and prices. There is even a dinner at the Eiffel Tower followed by a cruise on the Seine. You might meet some interesting people on the tour. If not, enjoy the sites, show and cuisine!

DAY 6

Morning Options

➢ Stroll through the Pantheon, Luxembourg
Gardens, Cluny, Maillol or Zadkine
museums, or take a walking tour of the
Left Bank. (Read explanations in your
Green Michelin if you are not taking
a tour.)

Afternoon Options

➢ Take a half-day tour to Chartres, a famous
medieval cathedral with magnificent
stained glass windows. Chartres is about
a 40-minute bus ride from Paris and the
tour takes about five hours. The other
choice is to go on your own; it is a half-
hour train trip.

➢ Take a half-day tour to Giverny, Monet's
home, with fabulous gardens and the
pond where he painted the water lilies.
Also about five hours or go on your
own (train about 40 minutes, then a 10-
minute taxi). *Remember — it is closed in
the winter.* Check the schedule with the
concierge.

➢ Take a walking tour of Montmartre.
Groups are small and guides are
knowledgeable.

➤ Take a leisurely stroll. Shop or visit museums like Marmottan, Nissim Camodo, Grand Palais or Petit Palais. Go up the Eiffel Tower or visit the art galleries on Rue Bonaparte, Rue des Beaux-Arts, and Rue de Seine. Shop the boutiques in the Marais District and do not forget Fauchon — the most elegant grocery store in the world.

➤ Sit at a café and finish writing all of your postcards plus your journal of your week in Paris

---

Evening Options

➤ Go out for a smashing good dinner (check restaurant list).

FINAL DAY

➤ Have the concierge call for a taxi. Plan to arrive at the airport two hours before your flight. Also, have the concierge reconfirm your flight the day before. Before leaving for the airport, go to one of the traiteurs (small delicatessen) and buy yourself a sandwich and a piece of fruit. (Airlines do not seem to serve lunch until around 3 p.m. and there is no need to starve while you are waiting.)

➤ When you arrive at the airport, ask the taxi driver to find a baggage cart for you. The word in French is chariot. Tip the driver 10 percent of the fare. Go directly to the check-in counter. Have your airline tickets and passport readily available. Be prepared to be patient! After checking in, if you have made any major purchases and were given tax refund forms from any stores, go directly to the tax refund desk. After stamping the forms, ask which form you keep. Place the other two forms in the stamped envelope and deposit in the mailbox that is usually right next to the tax refund desk.

➤ Next, keep your boarding pass, airline ticket and passport handy and proceed to customs. After clearing customs, enjoy a beverage or snack in one of the cafes or airline clubs. (If you are flying business or first class or are a regular member, the clubs are a comfortable, quiet oasis at the airport.) You also can do your duty free shopping at the wonderful boutiques in the Paris airport—just don't expect any great bargains. My favorite treat is buying smoked salmon. Proceed to your gate 45 minutes before departure. Again, keep your boarding pass, ticket and passport handy!

Au revoir Paris!

Two to Three Days Out From Paris

The Loire. Now that you have gotten a brief taste of Paris, it could be fun to spend a few days living the essence of historic France. The chateaux are castles of kings and nobility from the medieval ages through the 19th century. The kings and queens, lords and ladies of the court built imposing castles on the banks of the Loire River. Today they are historic monuments and can be visited for a fee (approximately $5 to $14). Some of the smaller ones still remain as private residences for descendants of the original owners. Today there are over 40 private chateaux in France that rent out two to eight bedrooms to guests. Usually, dinner is available with the family and other guests. It is like visiting your cousins in their large old country houses. They are all unique and furnished with various degrees of grandeur.

The *Bienvenue au Château* book available from the French Tourist Bureau has small pictures of the chateaux and lists the facilities that are available. Find one that fits your dreams and book a room for at least two days. Private chateaux that serve dinner are perfect for solo women. You have the family and a few other guests to return home to after a day of sightseeing the Grand Chateaux, vineyards and other historic sites.

86

Usually everyone gathers around 7 p.m. in the drawing room for aperitif (cocktails). Often madame (the owner) excuses herself to put finishing touches on dinner. You will be ushered into the dining room where you will feel like you are at a private dinner party in a very elegant setting. The host and hostess are generally very convivial and keep the conversation interesting and lively in English! Here you are received as an old friend. Loneliness, lack of language skills, fears of whatever all seem like distant unpleasant memories in these elegant but friendly settings.

Many of the private chateaux operate on a shoestring so do not expect a staff of servants. You will probably have to carry your own bag up to your bedroom, which actually takes the formality out and makes you feel more at home. Many are a bit run down; still all have modern conveniences such as private bathrooms and swimming pools, but lack air conditioning. If you do not travel in mid-July or August, this is not a problem.

Mid-July through the end of August is when all of Europe vacations, places are crowded, service is not up to par. You do not get your pick of hotels or rooms. Air conditioning is rare and unreliable. The best months for Europe are April, May, June, September and December.

Welcome Home: Customs

➤ Be polite to customs agents.

➤ Keep your purchases together in either a separate bag or in one compartment of your luggage.

➤ Have all of your bills together in one envelope that is readily accessible in your purse.

➤ Do not lie. The duty is so nominal — pay it with a smile.

➤ Do not wear flashy jewelry or clothes for traveling.

➤ When choosing a line for customs inspections try to stand behind corporate American types with leather attaché cases or grey haired tourists. They tend to clear customs quickly.

➤ Go home, unpack, relax. Remember it is six hours later for you. Try to stay awake until 9:30 or 10 p.m. Read your travel journal and savor all of your wonderful new experiences. Tomorrow you can start planning your next trip.

Be polite to your customs agent and
pay your duty with a smile.

How Not to
Go Through Customs

In February of 1995 the border between
Israel and Jordan had recently opened.
Travelers from Israel could enter Jordan
for the first time in 40 years, and the lost
Nabatean city of Petra could easily be visited from the Jordanian-Israeli border. I had
flown to Israel from Paris two days before,
arriving at the Jordanian border town of
Acquaba. I spent nearly three hours with
40 strangers waiting to pass through
Jordanian customs and begin our overnight
tour to Petra.

In my tote purse that I was using as an
overnight bag were the usual change of
travel clothes, cosmetic case and one small
hermetically sealed package of smoked
Petrossian salmon. (I adore smoked salmon.
It's half the price in France and I always
buy it whenever I am in Paris.) As I left my
hotel in Jerusalem for the trip to Petra, I
checked my luggage and went to leave my
salmon in the restaurant kitchen, but dis-
covered it was a very Orthodox religious
hotel. My salmon was forbidden in the
restaurant refrigerator. The cab was waiting
to take me to the airport for the short flight
to Elat, the Israeli border town with Jordan.
I grabbed my overnight bag, threw the
salmon in and left in a great tizzy.

After the flight and the interminable wait
at both the Israeli and Jordanian sides of

90

the border, I had completely forgotten about my fish. The Jordanian border guards finally called everyone up to the tables and told us to open our bags. The customs inspector went directly to me, looked through my bag and pulled out my package of salmon. He looked anxiously at my hermetically sealed plastic package and asked what it was. I told him it was a smoked fish from Paris. (The package was in its little Petrossian sack from Orly Airport.) The guard was furious with me for telling him this lump of plastic was a fish. He knew what a fish looked like. This lump did not have fins and a tail. Within moments my little smoked salmon and myself were surrounded by three men with machine guns. The 40 other tourists all turned deadly silent watching this Fellini-like fish story unfold.

I could not talk. I was afraid I would erupt into nervous, hysterical laughter. Someone came forward and explained to the guard in rapid Arabic about the Western process of smoking fish and sealing it. The chief of the station came out, examined it, and gingerly put it back into my bag. I ran onto the bus, where everyone applauded, and my fish and I were finally en route to Petra. Only the spectacle of entering Petra could match our auspicious entry to the Kingdom of Jordan. The combination of an unsophisticated customs official and an idiotic American tourist who was traveling with a fish in her purse will be retold for years by the 40 stunned international tourists.

HOW TO ORDER MORE BOOKS:

Going Like Lynn©

VISIT LYNN ON THE INTERNET:

Contact Lynn Portnoy via email:
goinglikelynn@womenbiz.net

Visit Lynn's website:
http://www.womenbiz.net/goinglikelynn

MAIL REQUESTS TO:

Lynn Portnoy
29260 Franklin Road
Suite 123
Southfield, MI 48034

TELEPHONE REQUESTS:

(248) 353-2900

If ordering by mail:

*Please include your name,
telephone number, shipping address
and number of books requested.
Make check payable to Lynn Portnoy.*

Cost: $12.95, plus $2.75 per book
(includes tax, shipping and handling)